LEVEL
1

Llamas

Maya Myers

NATIONAL GEOGRAPHIC

Washington, D.C.

To Mom and Dad, who always fed my curiosity.
—M. M.

Designed by Design Superette

The publisher and author gratefully acknowledge the expert content review of this book by George Barrington, DVM, PhD, professor of large animal medicine at the College of Veterinary Medicine at Washington State University, and the literacy review of this book by Mariam Jean Dreher, professor of reading education, University of Maryland, College Park.

Photo Credits
Cover, JeffGoulden/Getty Images; 1, Lindrik/Getty Images; 3, Eric Isselée/Shutterstock; 4-5, Harald Toepfer/Shutterstock; 6-7, vencavolrab/Getty Images; 8-9, George Steinmetz/National Geographic Image Collection; 9, LSP1982/Getty Images; 10, Laurent Davoust/Alamy Stock Photo; 11, G_Harvey/Getty Images; 12-13, Hugo Brizard-YouGoPhoto/Shutterstock; 14, tbradford/Getty Images; 15, Lisa Stelzel/Shutterstock; 16-17, Cezary Wojtkowski/Shutterstock; 18, Edwin Butter/Shutterstock; 19 (UP), burroblando/Getty Images; 19 (LO), Marcos Radicella/Getty Images; 20 (UP), Jeffrey Jackson/Alamy Stock Photo; 20 (LO), Gaston Aguilar/EyeEm/Getty Images; 21, Jose A. Bernat Bacete/Getty Images; 22 (UP), Frank Krahmer/Getty Images; 22 (CTR), John Moore/Getty Images; 22 (LO), Bob Elam/Alamy Stock Photo; 23 (UP LE), G. Lacz/Arco/Alamy Stock Photo; 23 (UP RT), Christian Heinrich/imageBROKER/Shutterstock; 23 (LO LE), Iakov Filimonov/Shutterstock; 23 (LO RT), Lisa Stelzel/Shutterstock; 24-25, imageBROKER/Shutterstock; 24 (INSET), Ami Vitale/National Geographic Image Collection; 26, Robert & Jean Pollock/Getty Images; 27 (UP), PERU Landmarks and People by Vision/Alamy Stock Photo; 27 (CTR), Paul Wishart/Zoonar/Alamy Stock Photo; 27 (LO), Cristina Stoian/Alamy Stock Photo; 28, hadynyah/Getty Images; 29, andresr/Getty Images; 30 (LE), aestang/Getty Images; 30 (RT), LFRabanedo/Shutterstock; 31 (UP LE), Christian Rummel/Getty Images; 31 (UP RT), Joel Matos/Shutterstock; 31 (LO LE), VisualCommunications/Getty Images; 31 (LO RT), Picture by Tambako the Jaguar/Getty Images; 32 (UP LE), Laurent Davoust/Alamy Stock Photo; 32 (UP RT), Lisa Stelzel/Shutterstock; 32 (LO LE), LSP1982/Getty Images; 32 (LO RT), imageBROKER/Shutterstock

Library of Congress Cataloging-in-Publication Data
Names: Myers, Maya, author. | National Geographic Society (U.S.)
Title: Llamas / by Maya Myers.
Description: Washington, DC : National Geographic Kids, [2020] | Series: National Geographic readers | Audience: Age 4-6. | Audience: K to Grade 3. | Identifiers: LCCN 2019007714 (print) | LCCN 2019008447 (ebook) | ISBN 9781426337277 (ebook) | ISBN 9781426337284 (e-book) | ISBN 9781426337253 (paperback) | ISBN 9781426337260 (hardcover)
Subjects: LCSH: Llamas--Juvenile literature.
Classification: LCC QL737.U54 (ebook) | LCC QL737.U54 M94 2020 (print) | DDC 599.63/67-- dc23
LC record available at https://lccn.loc.gov/2019007714

National Geographic supports K–12 educators with ELA Common Core Resources. Visit natgeoed.org/commoncore for more information.

Printed in the United States of America
19/WOR/1

Table of Contents

Take a Hike

Why are these llamas in the mountains? This is where they live! Llamas come from the Andes (AN-deez) Mountains.

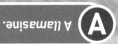

Llamas are made for mountain life. Their thick hair keeps them warm. Their long necks sway to help them balance on steep trails.

7

Family Matters

large herd

Llamas live in family groups called herds. Herds can be large or small.

small herd

Herd Word

HERD: A group of animals

The llamas in the herd
take care of one another.

Llamas compete
to be the most
powerful in the
herd. The dominant llama likes to
stand on higher ground than
the others.

Young llamas neck wrestle for fun. But when they are older, it can be a real fight!

11

Less than an hour after a baby llama is born, it can stand up and walk.

A baby llama is called a cria (KREE-uh).

But the baby will still need to stay close to its mother for about a year.

13

Llama Lunch

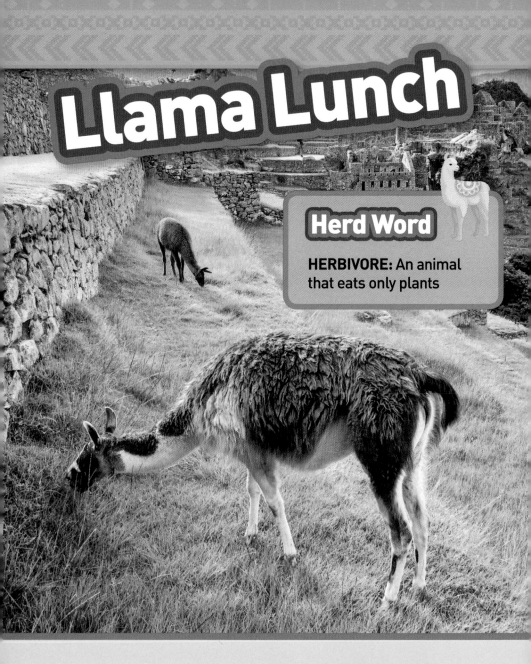

Llamas are herbivores (HER–buh–vorz). That means they eat only plants. They eat mostly grasses and hay.

Llamas chew their food, swallow it, then bring it back up to chew again.

Look at That Llama!

Llamas can weigh up to 440 pounds. That's more than some pianos! Most llamas are about as tall as an adult human. Let's take a closer look at llamas.

TAIL: Llamas use their tails to "talk" to other llamas.

FEET: Soft, padded feet help llamas keep steady on steep mountain trails and walk gently over farmers' fields.

NECK: A long neck helps llamas balance.

EARS: Llamas have excellent hearing. Their ears are shaped like bananas.

EYES: Their big eyes have long lashes to block bright light from the sun.

SNOUT: Big lips and long teeth make it easy to eat leaves and grass.

HAIR: Thick hair can be black, gray, white, or brown. It can be short or long. It keeps llamas warm.

TOES: Two long toes with sharp nails can grip rocky trails.

Llama Talk

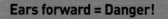
Ears forward = Danger!

Ears back = Get out of my space!

Llamas use their bodies to communicate (com-YUN-uh-kate). They move their ears to send messages.

The way they hold their tails means different things, too.

Stiff tail = Unhappy llama

Relaxed tail = Calm llama

Tall neck =
Large and in charge

Neck out = Look out!

Even the way a llama holds its neck
sends a signal to other llamas.

When they sense danger, llamas give a loud warning cry.

They also communicate by clucking, making a gargling sound, and humming.

21

7 FUN FACTS About Llamas

1 Llamas can throw tantrums! When they are very annoyed, they may spit, hiss, kick, and lie down. But usually they are friendly.

2 Therapy llamas visit with people who are sick or elderly.

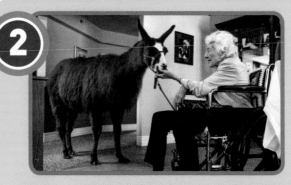

3 Llama poop doesn't stink! People use dried llama poop for fuel and fertilizer.

4 Llamas have been helping people for more than five thousand years. Llamas even helped people build the Inca city of Machu Picchu in Peru!

5 In Peru, lots of llamas have their ears pierced. People put tassels in to help tell them apart. They make good flyswatters, too!

6 Llamas are related to camels, but they are smaller and don't have humps.

7 Mama llamas hum to new babies, and their babies hum back!

Llamas at Work

Llamas are pack animals. They live with people and work to help them.

Herd Word

PACK ANIMAL: An animal that carries things for people

They use their strong bodies and sense of balance to carry heavy loads on steep mountainsides.

Llamas are smart and learn quickly. They can learn to protect herds of sheep or goats. If a dangerous animal comes close, the llama will scare it away.

This llama wool has not yet been spun into yarn.

This yarn is spun from dyed llama wool.

Llamas help people in other ways, too. People use llama wool to make cloth and rope.

The yarn can be used for weaving fabric on a loom.

Llama Love

Some people keep llamas as pets! They are very friendly and easy to train. They can learn new tasks and tricks after just a little practice (PRAK-tiss). You'd need a farm-size backyard, though!

What in the World?

These pictures are close-up views of llamas. Use the hints to help figure out what's in the pictures. Answers are on page 31.

1

HINT: These help block bright light.

2

HINT: A llama's foot has two of these.

Word Bank

toes   teeth   eyelashes   neck   tail   ear

3

HINT: This is shaped like a banana.

4

HINT: Llamas move this to "talk" to other llamas.

5

HINT: This helps with balance.

6

HINT: These help get food.

Answers: 1. eyelashes, 2. toes, 3. ear, 4. tail, 5. neck, 6. teeth

DOMINANT: Most powerful

HERBIVORE: An animal that eats only plants

HERD: A group of animals

PACK ANIMAL: An animal that carries things for people